ST WILLIAM'S
COLLEGE
The WORLD of the
MINSTER
SHOP &
RESTAURANT

"The
guidebook
that pays
for itself –
in one day"

York for less
How to use this book

This book enables 1 or 2 people to obtain discounts at a number of the best places in and around York.

To obtain discounts at different places, you must first validate this book by filling in the dates in the box opposite. Having done this, the following instructions apply:

Tours: follow the instructions on each page.

Attractions: hand over the relevant voucher from pages 51 to 60 when you pay for entrance. Circle on the voucher whether the discount applies for 1 or 2 people and whether they are adults, children, seniors or students.

Restaurants: show the waiter page 3 of this book when you ask for your bill to obtain a 25% discount off all food and beverage costs. The price range in the box under each entry is an *estimate* of the cost of a 2-course meal for one person. You receive the discount however much you spend.

Shops: show the cashier page 3 of this book before the price is rung up on the till to obtain a 20% discount off all goods. Discounts on goods that are already reduced in price are at the discretion of the shop's management.

Publisher Information

ISBN 1-901811-00-X

First published in Great Britain in 1997 by Metropolis International (UK) Limited, 222 Kensal Road, London, W10 5BN.

York for less
Contents

All discounts in this book are valid for up to 2 people for up to 4 consecutive days.

To obtain discounts you must first fill in the boxes below:

"STARTING DATE" box: the date you first use the card.
"ENDING DATE" box: the date <u>3 days after</u> the starting date.

STARTING DATE:
(DATE YOU FIRST USE THE CARD)
      __ / ___ / ___
      DAY / MONTH / YEAR

ENDING DATE:
(3 DAYS AFTER STARTING DATE)
      __ / ___ / ___
      DAY / MONTH / YEAR

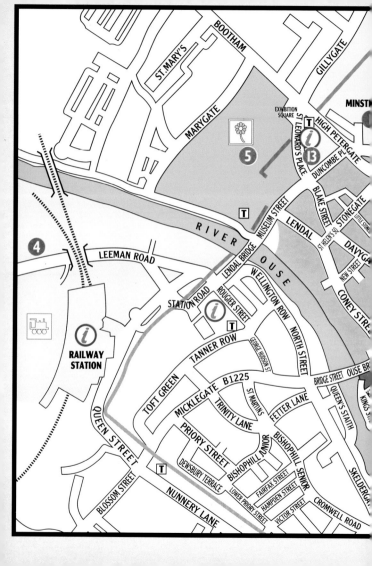

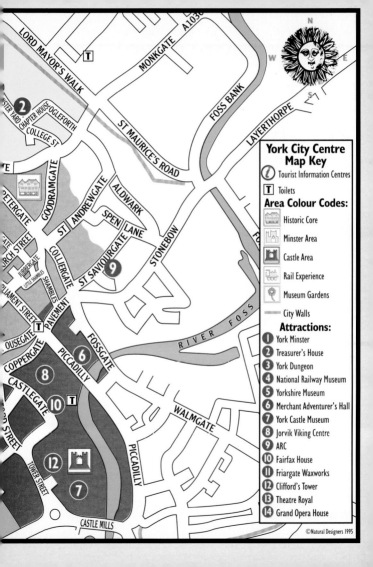

York
Introduction

One of the best preserved medieval cities in Europe, York remains remarkably unscathed by the huge influx of visitors who come to see its majestic cathedral, wander the medieval

alleys and enjoy the colourful street entertainers. Today, it is also a thriving modern city, with a lively student population, several major heritage sites and hundreds of delightful pubs and restaurants.

Street entertainers

From the **Roman** invasion of Britain until the industrial revolution, York was the most important city in the north of England. The Romans used it as a garrison town and two of their towers survive as part of the medieval walls. After the collapse of the Roman Empire, York became a regional capital first for the Saxons and then the Vikings.

Initially, the **Vikings** came to pillage, but eventually they settled and, more than 1,000 years ago, founded 'Jorvik'. The remains of the original Viking settlement have now been excavated and the **Jorvik Viking Centre** (page 26) is built over the Coppergate archaeological dig. Tools, clothing, utensils and other objects - all dating

Workman's bench - Jorvik Centre

back a millennium - are displayed. Visitors travel around in 'time capsules' past a reconstructed Viking settlement, with a busy market, a wharf and dark, smoky houses.

York
Introduction

The Scandinavian influence can best be seen today in the names of many of York's streets, which are known locally as 'gates', derived from the Norse word 'gata', meaning 'street'.

During the 13th and 14th centuries, the present city walls were built on top of the earlier Viking earthworks. The original purpose of these walls was to defend the town from attackers, and they were manned day and night. However, by the time the medieval walls were completed, the threat of foreign invasion had largely subsided.

The walls are punctuated by fortified gateways, the only entrances to the city, known as 'bars'. Each of these ancient gateways has its own colourful history and distinctive architecture. Thankfully, a public outcry saved the bars from demolition in 1832.

Mickelgate Bar

Bootham Bar, at the city's northern entrance, dates from the 12th century. It was through this gate that Roman soldiers would have entered their fortress from the north. The tallest gateway is **Monk Bar**, which has a working portcullis and carved stone figures on top.

Walmgate Bar is the best preserved of the bars, despite being damaged in the English Civil War. Bullet holes inflicted by Oliver Cromwell's troops after the Battle of Marston Moor in 1644 can still be seen in the stonework.

York
Introduction

Micklegate Bar, marking the approach from London, was the most important of the four main gates. The decapitated heads of traitors used to be displayed over the gate as a warning to others.

A walk along the scenic Bar Walls, which ring the historic heart of the city, offers a unique perspective of York. The full circuit takes two hours at a leisurely pace, though there are plenty of access points for a shorter walk.

York's Bar Walls

The section between Monk Bar and Bootham Bar affords the finest views of **York Minster** (page 25), the city's outstanding architectural jewel.

Built on the site of a Roman fortress, the 800-year-old Minster is the largest Gothic cathedral in northern Europe. Its official name is the Cathedral and Metropolitan Church of St. Peter, and it is the seat of the Archbishop of York, the second most important figure in the Church of England.

Interior of the Minster

Entrance to the main building is free (donations are appreciated). With this book, you can obtain a discount on the entrance to the foundations (page 25).

York
Introduction

Work on York Minster began in 1220, but the plans were so ambitious that it took 260 years to complete. The result is a medley of architectural styles, from the Early English octagonal Chapter House (1241-60) to the Perpendicular choir (1450).

The Minster is renowned for its magnificent stained glass windows, said to contain half of all the medieval stained glass in England. The Five Sisters Window remains from the late 1200s and is the cathedral's oldest complete window.

The Great West Window, dating from 1338, is known as the 'Heart of Yorkshire' because of its decorative heart-like shapes. Created almost 70 years later, the Great East Window depicts the biblical stories of Genesis and Revelations and, at 78ft by 31ft, is thought to be the largest medieval window anywhere in the world.

The Minster in snow

The Rose Window, in the south transept, contains 17,000 pieces of glass depicting scenes commemorating the marriage in 1486 of Henry VII and Elizabeth of York. Their marriage brought to an end the **War of the Roses**.

The top of the Central Tower offers the best rooftop view of York. Moving from top to bottom, the remains of previous Roman and Norman buildings can be seen in the Minster's foundations. In the late 1960s, huge concrete collars and six miles of reinforced steel rods were installed in the foundations after surveyors discovered that the Minster's central tower was on the verge of collapse. Many archaeological treasures were unearthed during the work on the foundations, and these are displayed in the Crypt and Treasury.

Having removed the threat of collapse, disaster of a different sort struck in 1984, when lightning sparked a fire in the Minster's roof. In the intense heat, the Rose Window shattered into thousands of fragments. It has now been painstakingly restored.

Treasurer's House at night

The **Treasurer's House** (page 31), located behind the Minster, has an intriguing confusion of architectural styles, ranging from Roman to Victorian. Built upon 12th-century foundations, the building itself dates back to the early 17th century. During the summer, the interior is open to the public. Pictures and furniture are on display as well as an exhibition about the Treasurers, the Minster's accountants. Beware of the basement, however, as it is said that the ghosts of long-deceased Roman auxiliary soldiers can still be seen here, marching along the old Roman road on top of which the Treasurer's House was built.

Near the Minster, you can visit the timber-fronted structure known as **St. William's College**, owned by the cathedral since the 15th century. It was the residence for chantry (singing)

priests throughout the 15th and 16th centuries. Today, you can walk through its medieval halls and visit York's brass-rubbing headquarters.

The **Yorkshire Museum** (page 29), west of the Minster, displays Roman, Viking and medieval treasures, including a reconstructed Roman kitchen, as well as a natural history collection. The

St. William's College

beautiful **Museum Gardens** contain ruins from many of York's eras, most importantly the 11th-century remains of **St. Mary's Abbey**. To learn about the science of archaeology in a fun and friendly environment, visit the **Archaeological Resource Centre** (page 27).

The **Assembly Rooms**, on Blake Street, were built between 1732 and 1736 by the third Earl of Burlington in order to provide a location for the city's social elite to hold their grand balls. At the time, the architecture of the pillar-lined Egyptian Hall met

with a great deal of criticism for being too dark and narrow. The Duchess of Marlborough described the forest of columns as resembling 'a row of ninepins'.

As a significant trading centre, York profited most from the

Relaxing in Museum Gardens

York
Introduction

wool trade. A weavers' guild was established as early as the 12th century and, in subsequent years, the riverfront Gothic **Guildhall** was used as a common meeting place. Unfortunately, an air raid in 1942 caused tremendous damage to the structure which has since been largely replaced. A plaque given by New York in 1924 was placed at the Guildhall in recognition of its namesake.

Clifford's Tower

Another fascinating historic building is the **Merchant Adventurers' Hall** (page 33) between Piccadilly and Fossgate, one of the best preserved medieval buildings in Europe. Dating back to the 14th century, this timbered building contains a collection of Elizabethan portraits, silver and furniture.

At the southern end of the walled city, on a high mound, stands the impressive **Clifford's Tower**. Steeped in history, the tower grew from one of two wooden castles beside the River Ouse founded by William the Conqueror in order to help overawe the northern tribes. After the original tower was destroyed by fire during the anti-Jewish riots of the late 12th century, the present four-sectioned structure, known as a quatrefoil, was rebuilt by Henry III.

Beside the tower is the **Castle Museum** (page 28) which re-creates Victorian and Edwardian interiors and street scenes.

York
Introduction

Housed in two 18th-century buildings, the museum contains the eccentric collection of Dr John Kirk, who gathered everyday items used in rural areas in the early years of the 20th century. The collection offers a unique history of the changing objects of everyday life and popular culture, including some of the first mass-produced televisions.

Shambles

Castlegate, round the corner from the Castle Museum, is a wonderful place to explore the elegance of York's Georgian period. **Fairfax House** (page 32), dating from the mid-18th century, is one of the finest Georgian townhouses in England and is acclaimed for its carved stucco ceilings and woodwork. On display is the exquisite furniture of the Terry family, who made a fortune from selling sweets, especially chocolates.

Shambles and **Stonegate**, both little-changed from medieval times in terms of structure, are two of the prettiest shopping streets in York. Shambles is still lined with craftsmen's shops which lean precariously towards each other. At its southern end is York's first paved street, appropriately named Pavement. Stonegate, originally the Via Pretoria of Roman York, abounds with modern gift shops and ancient pubs like Ye Olde Starre

Foss Bridge, Fossgate

Inne. The narrow medieval passages running between the streets are known as 'snickelways'.

More than 100 ghosts are rumoured to haunt the old town of York, and the winding streets and narrow passageways provide

City street signs

a suggestive backdrop for such tales. At a pub called the York Arms, numerous sightings have been reported, and objects such as cutlery and tableware are said to have moved around the rooms 'unguided by human hand'.

Many of the more lurid ghostly tales associated with ancient sites in York are related on several ghost-themed walking tours (pages 22-24).

Graphic representations of torture and execution are the big draws of **York Dungeon** (page 34) in Clifford Street. The final exhibit recreates the Gunpowder Plot of 1605, when York native Guy Fawkes tried to blow up the Houses of Parliament in London.

A good way to get around York and to see the sights is to go on the **Guide Friday** tour (page 20). It provides a fine overview of the town and helps visitors to choose a starting point for a walking tour, the best way to discover York's winding streets.

Cycle hire is also popular among visitors to York, with several companies offering daily rentals, including **York Cycle Hire** (Fetter Lane), **Bob Trotter** (Close to Monk Bar) and **Time Cycles** (17 Piccadilly).

York
Introduction

Along the River Ouse, you will find opportunities for river cruises, boat tours and motor boat hire.

York has a wide variety of places to eat, ranging from old-world favourites such as **Rockwell Rooms** (page 37), York's first covered tea-rooms and restaurant, to modern British cuisine at **The Deanery** (page 40). There are also several restaurants with tables overlooking the river, and a few pubs around the Ouse Bridge. Stonegate is popular for 'pub crawls', with a couple of bars offering live music.

The principal theatre is the **York Theatre Royal** (☎ 01904-623568), which stages both touring and home-grown plays and musicals.

Tourist Information Centres can be found at the bus and train stations. The main Information Centre is at Bootham Bar (De Grey Rooms, Exhibition Square, ☎ 01904-621756).

Located between London and Edinburgh, York is a popular stopover for travellers. Regular trains to both destinations take a little over two hours. For information on times and prices call **National Rail Enquiries** (☎ 0345-484950). For regional and long distance bus services, call the **Yorkshire Coastliner** (☎ 01653-692556) or **National Express** (☎ 01532-460011).

Take a cruise on the Ouse

York
History

The first major settlement in York was a fort established by the **Romans** in AD71-73. It was called **Eboracum**, a name derived from the Celtic word for 'the place of yew trees'.

Set up as a garrison town at the confluence of the River Ouse and River Foss by the 9th legion, the fort's purpose was to tame the wild northern territory of Britain.

Over time, Eboracum became the Roman capital of Lower Britain, second only to London in political and military significance.

In the 3rd century AD, Eboracum was a flourishing Roman colony protected by 4,000 troops. The town's rivers played a major role in establishing its pre-eminence in trade and commerce.

Roman remains -
The Multangular Tower (c.300AD)

It was one of the grandest fortresses in the Roman Empire, complete with stone walls, turrets and towers. It was here that Emperor Constantine Chlorus died in 306 and where his son, **Constantine the Great**, the first Christian emperor, divided Britain into four provinces, one of which had York as its capital.

However, in 410, the Roman army stationed at York abandoned the town and returned to Italy to help defend Rome from the barbarian invasions.

Eboracum's history in the 5th and 6th centuries is unclear.

York
History

During this time, it was invaded and seized by the **Saxons** who named it **Eoforwic**. In 625, Edwin, the King of Northumbria was married to Ethelburga, the Christian daughter of the King

of Kent. Two years later, King Edwin accepted Christianity and was baptized. The baptism took place in the wooden Church of St. Peter the Apostle, on the site of which York Minster now stands.

By 735, Christianity had taken root and the Pope honoured the city by sending an archbishop to oversee religious matters.

Anglian Helmet

The Danish **Vikings** defeated the Saxons in 867, burnt the city and renamed it **Jorvik**. It became their British capital for nearly 100 years and its population reached 10,000 people. During this time, the city again became a prominent trading centre.

Following an uprising against **Norman** rule in 1070, **Willam the Conqueror** burnt York to the ground and destroyed much of the surrounding countryside. He then rebuilt the city, constructing **Clifford's Tower** as a defensive stronghold.

During the medieval period, York became a prosperous port city . Wool

Inside Clifford's Tower

became the city's chief commodity and craftsman and merchants established guilds that would last for over 500 years.

The building of today's Minster was begun in 1220. Completed two and a half centuries later, in 1472, it is Britain's largest Gothic cathedral and is considered to be one of the finest architectural achievements of the Middle Ages.

Medieval York became a favoured royal retreat for the **Plantagenets**. Its importance was reflected in the creation of the title **Duke of York**, which has been bestowed ever since on the monarch's second son, including the present Duke of York, Prince Andrew. During this time, York remained the major military stronghold in the North and a major defence against marauding forces from Scotland.

Medieval entertainers

During the reign of **Henry VIII**, a number of York's fine medieval religious houses were destroyed during the **Dissolution of the Monasteries**. In protest at the Dissolution, Robert Aske led a band of rebels on the **Pilgrimage of Grace** and stormed the city. In 1537, the King's Council, a judicial body set up in the North, was reinstated and Aske was hung from Clifford's Tower.

During the 17th century, the city increased its wealth and national prominence. Indeed, Charles I uprooted the royal court from London and moved it to York. In the **Civil War**, Oliver Cromwell's Parliamentarians defeated the Royalists at the

York
History

Battle of Marston Moor, which took place six miles west of York, and captured the city.

A Georgian townhouse

Luckily, Sir Thomas Fairfax, leader of the Parliamentarians, was a local man who possessed a keen sense of history and saved many of York's architectural treasures from pillage, including the Minster.

During the Georgian period, the city flowered again, and became noted for its fashionable shopping streets and grand townhouses. With the introduction of stage coach travel from York to London in 1703, the city consolidated its position as the North's social and intellectual centre. During this period York was the home of several great writers, including **Laurence Sterne**, who published his satirical novel, *Tristram Shandy*, in Stonegate in the 1760s.

The Georgian Mansion House

In the 19th century, York became an important centre for the railway industry, but escaped the blights of industrialization.

In the 20th century, Yorkshire's commercial centre has moved away from York to larger industrial cities such as Leeds and Bradford. Today, York is an extremely beautiful, genteel city popular with visitors from all over the world.

Guide Friday
Open-Top Bus Tour

De Grey Rooms, Exhibition Square. ☎ 01904-640896

The Guide Friday open-top bus tour is one of the best ways to see York.

The green and cream buses follow a circular route which passes all the major tourist attractions. You can join or leave the bus at any stop and simply catch the next bus that comes along. In total, the tour takes one hour.

Throughout the tour, the trained guide will give you a fascinating commentary on the places which you are passing and the bus itself offers an excellent vantage point from which to take photographs of the passing city.

Main pickup points are the Railway Station, Museum Gardens, Exhibition Square and Clifford's Tower.

All year round. Summer from 9.20am running every 10 mins until 5pm. Less frequent out of season. No credit cards on bus. Adult £7, Child £2, Senior £5.50, Student £5.50. £3 off per person (child goes free) with voucher on page 51.

Castle Line Cruises
Boat Tours

Skeldergate Bridge, next to The Bonding Warehoouse.

Castle Line Cruises operate two ships, *The Duchess of York* and *The Empress*. They offer three different types of cruise from mid-March to the end of October.

'Hour Long Cruises' (which depart at 10.30am, 12.15pm, 1.30pm, 2.45pm, 4pm and 5.15pm) sail through historic York and out into the countryside. During the journey you listen to an historical commentary from the captain of the boat.

'Lunch Time Cruises' leave at 12.30pm and take you on a three-hour, ten-mile cruise through York, past the Bishops Palace to The Ship Inn. You pause here for one hour for lunch.

'Floodlit Evening Cruises' depart at 7pm and follow the same route as the Lunch Time Cruises with dinner at The Ship Inn.

Hour cruises: Adult £2.50, Child £1.50, Senior & Student £2.25. Lunch cruises: Adult £3.95, Child £2, Senior & Student £3.45 . Evening cruises: Adult £5.95, Child £2, Senior & Student £5.45. 50% off with voucher on page 51. No discount off food.

Ghost Trail of York
Walking Tours

☎ 01904-633276

 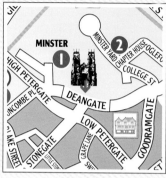

The Ghost Trail takes you back in time to experience the stories that make up the hidden and blood-chilling history of York's ghostly past.

Traditional tales, Victorian tragedies and true accounts of modern-day ghostly phenomena are all recounted as you walk around York's haunted places.

But do not relax too much, for in the shadows lurk dark figures who might join you at any moment and disturb you with their unwanted, evil presence.

The Ghost Trail of York is both an enjoyable stroll around the beautiful city and a spine-tingling experience that will haunt you forever.

Tours leave every evening at 7.30pm from the main doors of the Minster.
No credit cards accepted. Adult £3, Child £2, Senior £2.50, Student £2.50.
£1 off with voucher on page 59.

A Walk with Death
Walking Tours

☎ 01759-318778

Based on historical fact and eyewitness accounts, 'A Walk with Death' is a fascinating city tour that offers the opportunity to explore the darker side of York's history.

This entertaining tour takes a look at happenings in York in the last 600 years, including its executions, murder mysteries, abbeys, monks, dungeons, plagues, highwaymen and much more.

Walk the cobbled medieval streets and visit historical buildings that have played a role in earning York its macabre reputation.

Costumed guides and characters skillfully recount the heart-stopping, gruesome tales of death and torture that were once part of the city's culture.

Tours leave every evening at 7pm from the side of the Castle Museum by Clifford's Tower. No credit cards accepted. Adult £3.50, Child £2.50, Senior £3.00, Student £3.00. 50% off with voucher on page 59.

Original Ghost Walk
Walking Tours

Kings Arms Pub, Ouse Bridge. ☎ 01904-764222.

The Original Ghost Walk of York offers a fun but authentic opportunity to discover the magic of ancient York.

Using the rich language of the traditional storyteller, the qualified guides evoke the history of one of Britain's most haunted cities.

Established over 25 years ago, the guides helped to investigate and study some of Britain's strangest and most mysterious events.

Many of York's pubs and hotels have allegedly been visited by ghosts and popular tales include the ghost of the Minster, the child trapped in the plague house, the Roman soldiers in the Treasurer's House and the headless ghost of the Holy Trinity.

Tours leave every evening at 8pm from the Kings Arms Pub on Ouse Bridge.
No credit cards accepted. Adult £3, Child £2, Senior £3, Student £3.
£1 off with vouhcer on page 59.

York Minster

Minster Yard. ☎ 01904-624426

York Minster is the largest medieval building in England and the biggest cathedral north of the Alps.

A brilliant example of Gothic architecture, the Minster has dominated the city for eight centuries.

Entrance to the main body of the Minster is free and is a must for all visitors to York. A visit to the Central Tower, for which you pay, involves a long climb, but offers excellent views over the city.

The Foundations museum under the Minster (for which you are eligible for a discount) shows how the present building was constructed on the site of the Norman cathedral, which was itself built on a Roman fort.

York Minster: Mon-Sun: 7am-6pm (sometimes 8.30pm). Entrance is free.
Foundations: Mon-Sun: 10am-4.30pm (sometimes 6.30pm). No credit cards accepted. Adult £1.80, Child 70p. 50p off with voucher on page 51.

Jorvik Viking Centre

Coppergate. ☎ 01904-643211

Jorvik is a part of Viking York uncovered by archaeologists beneath Coppergate. As they removed the debris of centuries, houses and workshops emerged, still containing everyday tools and clothing from a civilisation buried for a thousand years.

Step aboard a 'time capsule' and travel through the reconstruction of a complete Viking settlement.

A bustling market, dark, smoky houses and a busy wharf have all been recreated in accurate detail so that you can experience in sight, sound and smell what it was like to live and work in Jorvik.

You also see preserved 10th-century buildings, standing where they were discovered during the archaeological dig.

Open Mon-Sun. 1 Apr-31 Oct: 9am-7pm. 1 Nov-31 Mar: 9am-5.30pm.
AM/VS/MC/DC. Adult £4.95, Child £3.60, Senior £4.60, Student £4.60.
25% off with voucher on page 51.

Archaeological Resource Centre

St. Saviourgate. ☎ 01904-654324

Located in the beautifully restored medieval church of St. Saviour, the Archaeological Resource Centre (ARC) is an award-winning hands-on exploration of archaeology for visitors of all ages.

It displays actual finds in a way that encourages visitors to become involved in archaeology. Visitors are allowed to touch and examine Viking and other artefacts.

You can also try your hand at the ancient crafts of spinning, weaving and leatherworking using traditional materials.

Modern technology is utilised to bring the process of archaeological discovery to life with computers, colourful graphics and touch access screens.

Mon-Fri: 10am-4pm. Sat: 1pm-4pm. Sun: closed. Last admission 3.30pm.
AM/VS/MC/DC. Adult £3.50, Child £3.50, Senior £3.50, Student £3.50.
25% off with voucher on page 53.

Castle Museum

The Eye of York. ☎ 01904-653611

The Castle Museum is one of the most popular museums of everyday life in Britain. Founded in 1938, it recreates different historical periods with detailed sets that are made up of original articles.

The best known reconstruction is of Victorian Kirkgate (pictured above), which was built by the founder of the museum.

Another life-size street called Half Moon Court represents life in Edwardian York. Thornley Park is a recreation of a typical Edwardian park.

In addition, there are period rooms and a modern collection called 'Every Home Should Have One' which displays early TV sets, vacuum cleaners and other household objects.

Apr-Oct: Mon-Sat: 9.30am-5.30pm. Sun: 10am-5.30pm. Nov-Mar: Mon-Sat: 9.30am-4pm. Sun: 10am-4pm. AM/VS/MC. Adult £4.50, Child £3.15, Senior £3.15, Student £3.15. Adult £1 off, others 50p off with voucher on page 53.

Yorkshire Museum

Museum Gardens. ☎ 01904-629745

The Yorkshire Museum houses one of Europe's richest archaeological collections, including some of the finest Roman, Anglo-Saxon, Viking and medieval treasures in Britain.

Rare artefacts include 2nd-century mosaics from York and a renowned Anglo-Saxon silver gilt bowl. Viking exhibits include the awesome warrior-stone from Weston.

Recently acquired for £2.5 million is the Middleham jewel (pictured above), the finest piece of English Gothic jewellery found this century.

The museum's beautiful grounds contain ten acres of botanical gardens, the remains of the Roman fortress walls and the ruins of St. Mary's Abbey.

1 Apr-31 Oct: Mon-Sun: 10am-5pm. 1 Nov-31 Mar: Mon-Sat: 10am-5pm. Sun: 1pm-5pm. Last admission 4.30pm. VS/MC. Adult £3.50, Child £2.25, Senior £2.25, Student £2.25. 50% off with voucher on page 53.

National Railway Museum

Leeman Road. ☎ 01904-621261

This is the largest and most comprehensive railway museum in the world. It offers a unique opportunity to learn about the history of rail transport.

Highlights include some of the original Royal Carriages, Stephenson's Rocket and the Mallard, the fastest steam locomotive in the world.

The story of the railways is also told through a constantly changing programme of special exhibitions, posters, paintings and artefacts, including lively audio-visual presentations.

For a light meal or refreshments, visit the Brief Encounter restaurant located in the South Hall. It offers hot and cold food together with teas, coffees and cakes.

Mon-Sat: 10am-6pm. Sun: 10am-6pm. Last admission 1 hour before closing.
AM/VS/MC/DC. Adult £4.80, Child £2.70, Senior £3.20, Student £3.20.
Adult £1 off, others 50p off per person with voucher on page 53.

Treasurer's House

Minster Yard. ☎ 01904-624247

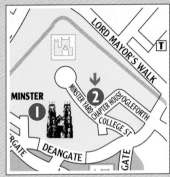

Situated in the heart of the city, beneath the towers of York Minster, this fascinating house is steeped in history.

Originally the home of the Minster's Treasurer, who controlled the Minster's finances, the building dates largely from the 17th century.

The radical reconstruction work undertaken by Frank Green, owner of the house at the end of the 19th century, has left a somewhat complicated architectural legacy.

As one moves from room to room, the interior design changes from elegant Georgian to opulent Victorian. Among the many highlights of the house are the tapestry room and two ornate lavatories that date from the turn of the century.

1 Apr-31 Oct: Mon-Thu and Sat-Sun: 10.30am-5pm. Last admission 4.30 pm.
Fri: closed. Nov-Mar: closed. No credit cards accepted. Adult £3.30, Child £1.65,
Senior £3.30, Student £3.30. £1 off with voucher on page 55.

Fairfax House

Castlegate. ☎ 01904-655543

Fairfax House offers a rare opportunity to experience the elegance of a Georgian townhouse.

It is one of the finest 18th-century townhouses in England. However, despite its obvious architectural merit, it was neglected and misused for many years.

Indeed, in this century it was used first as a cinema and then as a dance hall before being restored to its former glory by the York Civic Trust.

In addition to the superbly decorated plasterwork, wood and wrought iron, the house is now the home of an outstanding collection of 18th-century furniture and clocks which ensure that it is fully furnished in the style of the day.

Mon-Thu & Sat: 11am-4.30pm. Sun: 1.30pm-4.30pm. Fri: closed. Early Jan-mid Feb:closed. No credit cards accepted. Adult £3.50, Child £1.50, Senior £3, Student £3. Adult £1 off, others 50p off per person with voucher on page 55.

Merchant Adventurers' Hall

Piccadilly / Fossgate. ☎ 01904-654818

Built in 1357-62, the Merchant Adventurers' Hall is the finest medieval guild hall in Europe. Remarkably, its basic structure remains unaltered.

In the great timbered upper room, the merchants transacted their business, as their successors still do today. Below is their hospital for the poor with its own chapel.

There are collections, dating from Elizabethan times, of portraits, silver, furniture, banners, weights and measures, and other items used by the guild over the centuries. There are also exhibitions on the history of trade and guilds.

Leaflets are available in Dutch, French, German, Italian and Spanish.

15 Mar-8 Nov: Mon-Sun: 8.30am-5pm. 10 Mar-13 Nov: Mon-Sat: 8.30am-3pm. Sun: closed. Closed: 22 Dec-3 Jan. No credit cards accepted. Adult £1.90, Child 60p, Senior £1.60, Student £1.60. 50% off with voucher on page 55.

York Dungeon

12 Clifford Street. ☎ 01904-632599

The York Dungeon takes you back to a time before English society became genteel and ordered, to a time when execution and torture were everyday events.

Learn of the grisly punishments of branding, boiling, beheading, roasting and drowning.

Then unravel the truth about the local highwayman Dick Turpin and see him in the midst of a hold-up.

A special exhibit vividly recreates the Gunpowder Plot of 1605. You see the conspirators planning their mission and the arrest of Guy Fawkes (a native of York), followed by his terrible torture and execution for attempting to blow up the Houses of Parliament and the king.

Open Mon-Sun. Oct-Mar: 10am-4.30pm. Apr-Sep: 10am-5.30pm.
Last admission 1 hour before closing. VS/MC. Adult £4.45, Child £2.95,
Senior £3.45, Student £3.45. £1 off with voucher on page 55.

Murton Park

Murton Lane. ☎ 01904–489966

Opened in 1981, Murton Park has expanded to contain three different attractions, all ideally suited for children, in one location.

The Yorkshire Museum of Farming contains livestock and machinery displays, while the Children's Farmyard allows children to get close to the animals.

Danelaw Village re-creates Viking, Saxon and medieval lifestyles through a Dark Age village setting and a variety of unique programmes.

In the café, you can sample homemade food in a replica farmhouse kitchen. On Sundays and bank holidays, train rides are available on the Derwent Valley Light Railway.

Easter-Oct: Mon-Sun: 10am-5pm. Oct-Easter: Mon-Sun: 10am-4pm. No credit cards accepted. Adult £2.80, Child £1.50 (under 5 free), Senior £2.20, Student £2.20. 2 admissions for the price of 1 with voucher on page 57.

The Bar Convent Museum

17 Blossom Street. ☎ 01904-643238

Located in a charming Georgian building, the Bar Convent Museum recounts the early history of Christianity and its development in the North of England.

It also illustrates the life of Mary Ward, founder of the Institute of the Blessed Virgin Mary and a leader in women's education.

The Bar Convent contains a gallery, an audio-visual room and a 1769 neo-classical chapel with unique features, such as a priest hole and nine exits for quick escape, designed to protect the congregation during the days when Catholic worship was forbidden.

Adjacent to the courtyard is a shop and café, which serves light refreshments such as teas, biscuits and cakes.

Mon-Fri: 9.30am-5pm (last admission 4pm). Sat-Sun: closed. No credit cards accepted. Admission to museum & galleries: Adult £2, Child (under 16) £1, Senior £1.50, Student £1.50. 50% off with voucher on page 57.

Rockwell Rooms
Tea-Rooms & Restaurant

Stonegate Walk
☎ **01904-631399**

Rockwell Rooms are York's first covered tea-rooms and restaurant.

Both floors have an informal and relaxed atmosphere.

The comprehensive menu includes vegetarian dishes.

> Oct-Jun: Mon-Sun: 9am-5.30pm. Jul-Sep:
> Mon-Sun: 9am-9.30pm. AM/VS/MC/DC. £5-10.
> 25% off.

Russells
Traditional English

34 Stonegate
☎ **01904-641432**

Russells is best known for the succulent roasts served from its carvery.

Dine in Victorian elegance in York's most picturesque street.

You will not find better traditional English food in York.

> Mon-Sun: 10am-9.30pm.
> AM/VS/MC/DC. £10-15.
> 25% off.

Russells
Traditional English

26 Coppergate
☎ 01904-644330

This restaurant serves a wide selection of freshly prepared starters and sweets.

Here you eat in comfort under the beams of a 16th-century coaching inn.

Russells is also a great place to come for morning coffee or afternoon tea.

> Mon-Sun: 10am-9.30pm.
> AM/VS/MC/DC. £10-15.
> 25% off.

Cleopatra Coffee Bar
Café

4/5 Stonebow
☎ 01904-647536

Cleopatra Coffee Bar is an inexpensive place for a snack or quick meal.

Food served ranges from sandwiches to typical English dishes.

The décor is bright and modern with an Egyptian theme.

> Mon-Sat: 7.30am-5.30pm. Sun: closed.
> No credit cards accepted. £5-10.
> 25% off.

St. William's
Traditional English

College Street
☎ 01904-634830

St. William's is located in a 15th century building opposite the Minster.

The food is of a quality that matches the beautiful surroundings.

A speciality is smoked haddock and spinach fish cakes.

> Mon-Sun: 10am-5pm, 6.30pm-10pm.
> VS/MC. £10-15.
> 25% off.

Go Down Restaurant
Bistro / Brasserie

15 Clifford Street
☎ 01904-640117

The Go Down Restaurant is a cosy basement brasserie.

In the evenings, live music is played from Wednesday to Saturday.

Try the deep fried Wensleydale cheese wrapped in bacon.

> Mon-Sat: 5.30pm-10.30pm
> Sun: closed. AM/VS/MC. £10-15.
> 25% off.

The Deanery
Modern British

Galtres Lodge Hotel, 54 Low Petergate
☎ **01904-622478**

The Deanery is a comfortable hotel restaurant near York Minster.

It is located in a Georgian brick building which has been tastefully restored.

A speciality is roast beef and Yorkshire pudding.

Sun-Fri: 11.30am-3pm, 5pm-9pm.
Sat: 11.30am-9.30pm. VS/MC. £10-15.
25% off.

The Judges Lodging
Traditional English

9 Lendal
☎ **01904-638733**

Built in 1710, the Judges Lodging is a family-run hotel and restaurant.

It serves traditional English food in elegant surroundings.

The *table d'hôte* menu is modestly priced, the à la carte has great variety.

Mon-Sat:11.30am-2.15pm, 5pm-9.30pm.
Sun: 12noon-2.15pm, 6.30pm-9.30pm.
AM/VS/MC/DC. £10-15. 25% off.

The Dean Court Hotel
Traditional English

Duncombe Place
☎ 01904-625082

The Dean Court Hotel serves modern and traditional English food.

It has a spacious dining room with superb views of the Minster.

The seafood dishes are highly recommended.

> Mon-Sun: 7am-9.30am, 12.30pm-2.30pm,
> 7pm-9.30pm. AM/VS/MC/DC. £10-15.
> 25% off.

Delifrance
French / Café

71 Low Petergate
☎ 01904-671977

Delifrance specialises in large filled French baguettes.

You can choose from a wide range of hot and cold fillings.

All bakery products are made daily on the premises.

> Mon-Sat: 8am-9pm. Sun: 9am-9pm.
> No credit cards accepted. £5-10.
> 25% off.

Whitehead and Schmitter
English / French

55 Goodramgate
☎ 01904-632734

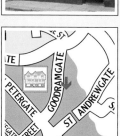

Whitehead and Schmitter is a great place to come for a quiet, relaxed meal.

It is situated in a traditional 16th-century building with exposed timbers.

The menu changes frequently and seafood dishes are a speciality.

> Mon-Fri: 11am-2pm, 6.30pm-9.30pm.
> Sat: 11am-3pm, 6.30pm-10pm. Sun: closed.
> VS/MC. £10-15. 25% off.

Bengal Brasserie
Indian

21 Goodramgate
☎ 01904-640066

Voted best restaurant of the year (1996) by the *Evening Post* newspaper.

Traditional Indian screens and pictures create a relaxed, authentic ambience.

Try the chef's specialities, the *murgh achar* or the excellent *gosh Bengal*.

> Mon-Fri: 12noon-2.30pm, 6pm-12midnight.
> Sat-Sun: 12noon-12midnight. VS/MC.
> £10-15. 25% off.

Bella Pasta
Italian

89 Low Petergate
☎ 01904-611221

Bella Pasta serves good-value Italian food from restaurants all over London.

Best known for its pasta dishes, it also serves great pizzas.

It is a great place to come for a reasonably priced dinner.

Mon-Sat: 10.30am-11pm. Sun: 12noon-10.30pm.
AM/VS/MC/DC. £5-10.
25% off with voucher on page 57-59.

Oscar's Wine Bar
Wine Bar & Bistro

8 Little Stonegate
☎ 01904-652002

Oscar's is a Continental-style wine bar and bistro.

The décor is old fashioned and the atmosphere is relaxed.

Try the 8oz burgers or the home cooked traditional lasagne.

Mon-Sat:11am-11pm. Sun: 12noon-10.30pm.
VS/MC. £5-10.
25% off.

Hamiltons
Old-fashioned Sweet Shop

24 Pavement
☎ 01904-629993

Step back in time to the days of Sherbet Lemons and Pear Drops.

Hamiltons also offers an extensive range of luxury hand-made chocolates.

It is a stockist of American Jelly Belly Beans and Bendicks of Mayfair.

> Mon-Sat: 9am-5.30pm. Sun: 10am-5.30pm.
> VS/MC.
> 20% off.

Forever Changes
Jewellery, Clothing & Gifts

42 Stonegate
☎ 01904-671243

Forever Changes is an Aladdin's cave of jewellery, clothing and gifts.

It is set in a very old building in the shadow of the Minster.

It imports directly from overseas and the prices are very competitive.

> Mon-Fri: 10am-5.30pm. Sat: 10am-6pm.
> Sun: 11am-5.30pm. AM/VS/MC/DC.
> 20% off.

English Teddy Bears
Bears & Clothing

36 Stonegate
☎ **01904-622822**

This shop sells a wonderful collection of hand-made English teddy bears.

It is popular with people of all ages and nationalities.

The teddies make a great gift for adults or for children.

> Mon-Sat: 10am-5.30pm. Sun: 11am-5pm.
> VS/MC.
> 20% off.

Beech Craft Designs
Prints

11 Grape Lane
☎ **01904-652230**

Beech Craft Designs sells a wide selection of framed prints.

Limited editions, local views and original watercolours are all stocked.

There is also a 24-hour picture-framing service.

> Mon-Sat: 9am-5pm. Sun: closed.
> AM/VS/MC.
> 20% off.

Artefact
Prints & Frames

42 Low Petergate
☎ 01904-639741

Artefact is a fascinating art shop located close to the Minster.

It stocks the widest selection of wall-to-wall prints in the North of England.

Whatever size of print you purchase, a frame can be fitted.

> Mon-Sat: 9.30am-5.30pm. Sun: 11am-4pm.
> VS/MC.
> 20% off.

Ilex
Natural Beauty Care

12 Stonegate
☎ 01904-640509

Ilex sells its own range of natural beauty products and pure essential oils.

None of the products have been tested on animals or have artificial ingredients.

They are suitable for the most sensitive skin and are reasonably priced.

> Mon-Sat: 10am-5pm. Sun: closed.
> AM/VS/MC/DC.
> 20% off. (no discount off Okra glass).

Definitely Different
Gifts

4 Pinders Court
☎ 01904-631856

Definitely Different sells original gifts, all hand-made in Britain.

Pet plants, flying pigs, wind chimes and freshly caught fairies are all sold.

The range of unusual items makes this a fascinating shop to visit.

Mon-Sun: 10am-5pm.
AM/VS/MC.
20% off.

Inglis and Son
Jewellers & Silversmiths

52 Stonegate
☎ 01904-654104

Established in 1866, Inglis is located in an historic building.

It is a high-class modern jewellers and silversmiths.

Watches, clocks, rings and other items of expensive jewellery are sold.

Mon-Sat: 10am-5pm. Sun: closed.
AM/VS/MC/DC.
20% off.

Blotter's
Stationery & Gifts

10 Church Street
☎ 01904-638518

Blotters stocks a variety of souvenirs and gifts suitable for all ages.

Seasonal items and greeting cards are also sold.

It is an ideal place to purchase a momento of your visit to York.

> Mon-Sat: 9am-5.30pm. Sun: closed.
> No credit cards accepted.
> 20% off.

Alan Stuttle Gallery
Pictures & Frames

50 Micklegate
☎ 01904-624907

Alan Stuttle is a well-established art gallery with its own resident artist.

It sells oil paintings, watercolours, prints and limited editions.

Its wide selection of original works appeals to people of all ages.

> Mon-Fri: 9.30am-5pm. Sat: 9am-5pm. Sun: closed.
> AM/VS/DC.
> 20% off.

Bath for less – £3.95
Valid for 2 people for 4 days

Come and see our unique Roman Baths and superb Georgian architecture and take advantage of great offers at attractions, shops and restaurants with *Bath for less*" - Paul Simons, Executive Director, Bath Tourism Bureau.

16 Attractions	- 10%-100% off
2 Tours	- 30%-50% off
16 Restaurants	- 25% off
6 Shops	- 20% off

Edinburgh for less – £3.95
Valid for 2 people for 4 days

'The *Edinburgh for less* book offers visitors great value at many of the city's top attractions, theatres, restaurants and shops. It will add to your enjoyment of Britain's most beautiful city' - Roger Carter, Chief Executive, Edinburgh Tourist Board.

12 Attractions	- 20%-70% off
2 Tours	- 20%-100% off
14 Restaurants	- 25% off
14 Shops	- 20% off

London for less - £12.95
Valid for 4 people for 8 days

London for less provides visitors with a guidebook, a fold-out map and a card that offers discounts at over 250 places.

45 Attractions	20%-50% off entrance
30 Tours and Car Rental	20%-50% off ticket prices
90 Restaurants	25% off food and beverages
50 Shops	20% off all goods
Shows and Orchestras	25%-70% off ticket prices

'**London for less** will help you make the most out of your stay in London by offering excellent savings on a wide range of our best places. Use it to explore and to enjoy yourself more, by day and by night' - Adele Biss, Chairman British Tourist Authority.

For more information about **Edinburgh for less, Bath for less, York for less** or **London for less**, please call Metropolis International (UK) Limited on 44-(0)181-964-4242.

Guide Friday (page 20)

No. of adults	1	2
No. of children	1	2
No. of seniors	1	2
No. of students	1	2

Circle as appropriate. Voucher valid for 1-2 people.

Castle Line Cruise (page 21)

No. of adults	1	2
No. of children	1	2
No. of seniors	1	2
No. of students	1	2

Circle as appropriate. Voucher valid for 1-2 people.

York Minster Foundations (page 25)

No. of adults	1	2
No. of children	1	2
No. of seniors	1	2
No. of students	1	2

Circle as appropriate. Voucher valid for 1-2 people.

Jorvik Viking Centre (page 26)

No. of adults	1	2
No. of children	1	2
No. of seniors	1	2
No. of students	1	2

Circle as appropriate. Voucher valid for 1-2 people.

This voucher entitles 1 or 2 people to a discount of £3 each off the price of a **Guide Friday Open-Top Bus Tour** (page 20). Children go free.

Voucher expires on December 31st, 1998

This voucher entitles 1 or 2 people to a discount of 50% each off the price of a **Castle Line Cruise** (page 21). No discount off food.

Voucher expires on December 31st, 1998

This voucher entitles 1 or 2 people to a discount of 50p each off entrance to **York Minster Foundations** (page 25).

Voucher expires on December 31st, 1998

This voucher entitles 1 or 2 people to a discount of 25% each off entrance to the **Jorvik Viking Centre** (page 26).

Voucher expires on December 31st, 1998

Archaeological Resource Centre (page 27)

No. of adults	1	2	Circle as appropriate. Voucher valid for 1-2 people.
No. of children	1	2	
No. of seniors	1	2	
No. of students	1	2	

Castle Museum (page 28)

No. of adults	1	2	Circle as appropriate. Voucher valid for 1-2 people.
No. of children	1	2	
No. of seniors	1	2	
No. of students	1	2	

Yorkshire Museum (page 29)

No. of adults	1	2	Circle as appropriate. Voucher valid for 1-2 people.
No. of children	1	2	
No. of seniors	1	2	
No. of students	1	2	

National Railway Museum (page 30)

No. of adults	1	2	Circle as appropriate. Voucher valid for 1-2 people.
No. of children	1	2	
No. of seniors	1	2	
No. of students	1	2	

This voucher entitles 1 or 2 people to a discount of 25% each off entrance to the **Archaeological Resource Centre** (page 27).

Voucher expires on December 31st, 1998

This voucher entitles 1 or 2 people to a discount of £1 (adult) or 50p (child, senior or student) each off entrance to the **Castle Museum** (page 28).

Voucher expires on December 31st, 1998

This voucher entitles 1 or 2 people to a discount of 50% each off entrance to the **Yorkshire Museum** (page 29).

Voucher expires on December 31st, 1998

This voucher entitles 1 or 2 people to a discount of £1 (adult) and 50p (child) each off entrance to the **National Railway Museum** (page 30).

Voucher expires on December 31st, 1998

Treasurer's House (page 31)

No. of adults	1	2
No. of children	1	2
No. of seniors	1	2
No. of students	1	2

Circle as appropriate. Voucher valid for 1-2 people.

Fairfax House (page 32)

No. of adults	1	2
No. of children	1	2
No. of seniors	1	2
No. of students	1	2

Circle as appropriate. Voucher valid for 1-2 people.

Merchant Adventurer's Hall (page 33)

No. of adults	1	2
No. of children	1	2
No. of seniors	1	2
No. of students	1	2

Circle as appropriate. Voucher valid for 1-2 people.

York Dungeon (page 34)

No. of adults	1	2
No. of children	1	2
No. of seniors	1	2
No. of students	1	2

Circle as appropriate. Voucher valid for 1-2 people.

This voucher entitles 1 or 2 people to £1 each off entrance to **Treasurer's House** (page 31).

Voucher expires on December 31st, 1998

This voucher entitles 1 or 2 people to a discount of £1 (adult) or 50p (child, senior or student) each off entrance to **Fairfax House** (page 32).

Voucher expires on December 31st, 1998

This voucher entitles 1 or 2 people to a discount of 50% each off entrance to **Merchant Adventurer's Hall** (page 33).

Voucher expires on December 31st, 1998

This voucher entitles 1 or 2 people to £1 each off entrance to the **York Dungeon** (page 34).

Voucher expires on December 31st, 1998

Murton Park (page 35)

No. of adults	1	2	Circle as appropriate. Voucher valid for 1-2 people.
No. of children	1	2	
No. of seniors	1	2	
No. of students	1	2	

The Bar Convent Museum (page 36)

No. of adults	1	2	Circle as appropriate. Voucher valid for 1-2 people.
No. of children	1	2	
No. of seniors	1	2	
No. of students	1	2	

Bella Pasta (page 43)

This voucher entitles up to 2 people to save 25% off the total bill (including food and beverages) at Bella Pasta.

Bella Pasta (page 43)

This voucher entitles up to 2 people to save 25% off the total bill (including food and beverages) at Bella Pasta.

This voucher entitles 1 person to a free admission to **Murton Park** (page 35) when 1 admission of equal or greater value is purchased.

Voucher expires on December 31st, 1998

This voucher entitles 1 or 2 people to a discount of 50% each off entrance to **the The Bar Convent Museum** (page 36).

Voucher expires on December 31st, 1998

Not valid in conjunction with any other offer. Voucher should be presented with bill before paying or discount cannot apply. Not redeemable for cash.

Voucher expires on December 31st, 1998

Not valid in conjunction with any other offer. Voucher should be presented with bill before paying or discount cannot apply. Not redeemable for cash.

Voucher expires on December 31st, 1998

Bella Pasta (page 43)

This voucher entitles up to 2 people to save 25% off the total bill (including food and beverages) at Bella Pasta.

Ghost Trail of York (page 22)

No. of adults	1	2
No. of children	1	2
No. of seniors	1	2
No. of students	1	2

Circle as appropriate. Voucher valid for 1-2 people.

A Walk With Death (page 23)

No. of adults	1	2
No. of children	1	2
No. of seniors	1	2
No. of students	1	2

Circle as appropriate. Voucher valid for 1-2 people.

Original Ghost Walk (page 24)

No. of adults	1	2
No. of children	1	2
No. of seniors	1	2
No. of students	1	2

Circle as appropriate. Voucher valid for 1-2 people.

Not valid in conjunction with any other offer. Voucher should be presented with bill before paying or discount cannot apply. Not redeemable for cash.

Voucher expires on December 31st, 1998

This voucher entitles 1 or 2 people to a discount of £1 each off the price of a **Ghost Trail of York** guided tour (page 22).

Voucher expires on December 31st, 1998

This voucher entitles 1 or 2 people to a discount of 50% each off the price of an **'A Walk With Death'** guided tour (page 23).

Voucher expires on December 31st, 1998

This voucher entitles 1 or 2 people to a discount of £1 each off the price of an **Original Ghost Walk** guided tour (page 24).

Voucher expires on December 31st, 1998

York for less customer satisfaction card

We would like to hear your comments about *York for less* so that we can improve the programme. Please complete the information below and mail this card to us. One card will be picked out at random and the winner will win a free London holiday. No stamp is required, either in Britain or your home country.

Name: ....

Address: ....

....

Where did you purchase *York for less*?...

....

Name of tour operator used? ....

Number of people travelling in your party? ....

How many days were you in York? ....

Which other British cities did you visit?..

....

Which other European cities did you visit?..

....

How much money did *York for less* save you? ....

Please circle which discounts you used:

attractions ~ *tours* ~ *shops* ~ *restaurants*

Did you like the guidebook and map?...

....

Would you recommend *York for less* to a friend?.................................

Any other comments / suggestions ....

....

....

....

....

NE PAS AFFRANCHIR

NO STAMP REQUIRED

By air mail
Par avion

IBRS/CCRI NUMBER: PHQ-D/2560/W

RESPONSE PAYEE
GRANDE-BRETAGNE

Metropolis International (UK) Limited
222 Kensal Road
LONDON
GREAT BRITAIN
W10 5BR

Notes

Notes